Essential COOKING SERIES

COMPREHENSIVE, STEP-BY-STEP COOKING

Finger Food

HINKLER
BOOKS

Essential Cooking Series: Finger Food
First published in 2009 by Hinkler Books Pty Ltd
45–55 Fairchild Street
Heatherton Victoria 3202 Australia
www.hinklerbooks.com

Disclaimer: The nutritional information listed under each recipe does not
include the nutrient content of garnishes or any accompaniments not listed
in specific quantitites in the ingredient list. The nutritional information for
each recipe is an estimate only, and may vary depending on the brand of
ingredients used, and due to natural biological variations in the composition
of natural foods such as meat, fish, fruit and vegetables. The nutritional
information was calculated by using Foodworks dietary analysis software
(Version 3, Xyris Software Pty Ltd, Highgate Hill, Queensland, Australia) based
on the Australian food composition tables and food manufacturers' data.
Where not specified, ingredients are always analysed as average or medium,
not small or large.

ISBN: 978 1 7418 5710 8

10 9 8 7 6 5 4 3
14 13 12 11 10

Printed and bound in China

Contents

An introduction to finger food

Whether it's to celebrate a birthday, a new house, a new year or just to gather together a group of friends and acquaintances, parties can be a source of such pleasure. Part of the pleasure at a party is the food. Imagine platters of lobster filo triangles circulating guests in tandem with Moroccan lemon shish kebabs or baked mushrooms. This book offers exciting finger food recipes to suit every taste and every occasion.

ORGANISATION

Long before the event, parties require considerable organisation. Decisions need to be made about venues, numbers, decorations, themes, invitations and, of course, food and drink. Planning your menu well ahead will minimise unexpected last-minute headaches. Think about types of food, quantities, cooking practicalities and serving utensils.

Firstly, do not rule out buying a few pre-made party foods, such as baby gourmet pies, satay sticks, spring rolls and Asian dumplings. They can be well-priced, good quality and readily available.

When you plan the menu, consider the size of your oven. If you plan too many hot dishes, you may have trouble finding oven space and the time to heat them all. It's also best if you cook things beforehand and only use the oven to warm things before serving. If you have frozen foods, defrost them in advance. It is also a good idea to serve cold dishes, such as dips and crudités, antipasto platters and cheese plates, as these do not require much preparation and can be made well ahead of time.

You will need plenty of platters. If it's a big party, you may need to hire some from a party hire store. You may also need to hire other things such as glasses and tables and chairs. Napkins should be placed onto each platter so guests can take a napkin with the food. Cocktail sticks or toothpicks might also be needed if you are serving meatballs. Place a few bins around the room for things such as bones or olive pips.

Finally, if it is a large party you may want to consider employing waiting staff to assist you. Hospitality agencies have experienced people who can help make your job easier. They can hand around food, top up guests' drinks and clean up the aftermath, giving you time to relax and enjoy the party.

TIMING

Timing is important. Dips and antipasto platters or cheese plates can be put out for when people arrive, allowing you time to greet your guests and fill their glasses. Once everyone has arrived you can begin warming and serving the food. It is often a good idea to alternate meat-based bites with vegetarian bites. Finally, unless your gathering is an afternoon tea or garden party, serve the sweet food last.

PRESENTATION

A little effort with presentation goes a long way. Decorating a platter with edible flowers such as nasturtiums can brighten up the whole room. Adding a small herb sprig to canapés will add extra colour. Serving bite-size treats on Chinese spoons or in a bamboo steamer will create an Asian vibe. Lining platters with paper doilies or banana leaves will stop food from sliding across the platter as you walk around the room.

HOW MUCH TO SERVE?

Not having enough food is every host's nightmare, and as a result most people tend to over-cater. The following is a rough guide to quantities:

PRE-DINNER NIBBLES
allow 3–5 pieces per person

FOR A 2–3 HOUR COCKTAIL PARTY
allow 4–6 pieces per person

FOR A PARTY WITH NO MAIN MEAL
allow 8–12 pieces per person

As a general rule, for up to 20 people you should plan 6 different dishes. For more than 20 people, you should consider 8–10 dishes.

For drinks

For a 2–3 hour cocktail party allow 1 bottle of wine between 2 people. White is usually more popular than red. If serving champagne, allow 3 glasses per person.

Always have soda, mineral water and soft drinks on hand. Buy plenty of ice and have lots of glasses – usually 2–3 per person depending on the occasion. If people are drinking beer and wine, attach a few bottle openers to a spot near where the drinks are being served.

INVITATIONS

Invitations can be used to inform people about what to expect. For instance, you can make it clear that you will be serving finger food, so that people do not arrive expecting a sit-down meal. Invites can also help with planning food. If you have any guests with special dietary requirements such as vegetarianism, remind them to let you know about it when they RSVP. Finally, don't forget to specify whether alcohol is provided or not.

Olive scones with thyme cured beef

INGREDIENTS

chutney of your choice
fresh thyme sprigs
thyme cured beef
185 g (6 oz) sugar
125 g (4 oz) salt
3 tablespoons crushed
  black peppercorns
1 large bunch (about 60 g, 2 oz)
  fresh thyme, leaves only
200 g (7 oz) lean beef fillet,
  trimmed of visible fat
olive scones
oil for greasing
250 g (8 oz) plain flour
2 teaspoons baking powder
45 g (1½ oz) black olives, chopped
1 tablespoon chopped fresh basil
freshly ground black pepper
1 cup (250 ml, 8 fl oz) buttermilk
1 tablespoon dijon mustard
makes 24 scones or
48 open-faced canapés

PREPARATION TIME
20 minute, plus
24 hour refrigeration

COOKING TIME
20 minutes

1 To cure beef: Place sugar, salt, peppercorns and thyme leaves on a large plate. Roll beef in mixture several times to coat and form a crust. Place beef on a wire rack set in a shallow dish. Cover and refrigerate for 24 hours, checking occasionally that the crust remains intact.

2 Using absorbent kitchen paper, thoroughly wipe away the herb crust. Using a sharp knife, cut beef across the grain into paper-thin slices – this is easier if you place the fillet in the freezer for 10 minutes before slicing. Place slices on a plate, cover and refrigerate until ready to use.

3 For the scones: Preheat oven to 200°C (400°F, gas mark 6). Lightly brush a baking tray with oil and set aside.

4 Into a large bowl, sift flour and baking powder. Add olives, basil and black pepper to taste. Mix to combine. Make a well in the centre. In a small bowl, place milk and mustard. Whisk to combine and pour into flour mixture. Mix quickly to make a soft dough. Turn dough onto a lightly floured surface. Knead lightly until smooth.

5 Press dough or roll out to form a 2 cm (¾ in) thick rectangle. Using a 3 cm (1¼ in) scone cutter, cut out scones. Place with sides just touching on prepared baking tray. Bake for 10–12 minutes or until scones are well risen and golden. Transfer to a wire rack. Cool slightly.

6 To serve, split scones and spread with a little chutney. Top with a small mound of beef and a thyme sprig.

NUTRITIONAL VALUE PER SERVE	FAT 3.3 G	CARBOHYDRATE 30.1 G	PROTEIN 5.1 G

Aubergine dip

INGREDIENTS

1 large aubergine (eggplant)
1 tablespoon lemon juice
2 medium tomatoes
3 tablespoons olive oil
1 medium onion, chopped
2 cloves garlic, crushed
$1/2$ teaspoon salt
$1/2$ teaspoon lemon pepper
$1/8$ teaspoon freshly ground
   black pepper
1 packet water crackers or
   toasted turkish bread
makes about 750 g (1$1/2$ lb)

1 To create the aubergine (eggplant) serving dish:
   Place the aubergine (eggplant) on its side and
   determine which side will serve as the base. Cut off
   the top side in a shallow slice and hollow out the
   flesh, leaving a 5–10 mm ($1/4$ – $1/2$ in) shell. Rub the
   edge of the shell with lemon juice, wrap it tightly
   and refrigerate.

2 Chop the aubergine (eggplant) flesh coarsely. Peel,
   seed and coarsely chop the tomatoes.

3 Heat olive oil in a large frying pan and sauté the
   aubergine (eggplant), tomatoes, onion and garlic
   on a medium–high heat for 5–6 minutes. Reduce
   heat, add the salt, lemon pepper and black pepper
   and simmer for 20–25 minutes. Remove the
   frying pan from heat and allow to cool to room
   temperature.

4 Place mixture in a food processor and process until
   combined. Refrigerate until needed.

5 When ready to serve, fill the reserved aubergine
   (eggplant) shell with dip and garnish with parsley.
   Serve with water crackers or toasted turkish bread.

PREPARATION TIME
15 minutes

COOKING TIME
30–35 minutes

NUTRITIONAL VALUE PER SERVE   FAT **5.7** G   CARBOHYDRATE **27.2** G   PROTEIN **4.7** G

Mini pizzas

INGREDIENTS

1 teaspoon active dry yeast
pinch sugar
²/₃ cup (170 ml, 5¹/₂ fl oz) warm
   water
250 g (8 oz) plain flour
¹/₂ teaspoon salt
4 tablespoons olive oil
classic pizza topping
185 g (6 oz) tomato paste
dried oregano leaves
315 g (10 oz) cherry tomatoes,
   sliced
125 g (4 oz) pepperoni or
   cabanossi, thinly sliced
20–25 pitted black olives,
   thinly sliced
250 g (8 oz) mozzarella cheese,
   grated
makes about 80

1 To make dough: In a small bowl, place yeast, sugar and water and mix to dissolve. Set aside in a warm place for 5 minutes or until mixture is foamy.

2 Place flour and salt in a food processor and pulse until combined. With machine running, slowly pour in yeast mixture and oil and process to make a rough dough. Turn dough onto a lightly floured surface and knead for 5 minutes or until soft and shiny. Add more flour if necessary.

3 Place dough in a lightly oiled bowl and roll around bowl to cover surface with oil. Cover bowl with plastic food wrap and place in a warm, draught-free place for 1–1¹/₂ hours or until doubled in size. Knock down and knead lightly.

4 Preheat oven to 190°C (375°F, gas mark 5). Divide dough into 4 cm (1¹/₂ in) balls, press out to make 7 cm (3 in) circles and place on greased baking trays. Spread each dough circle with tomato paste, then sprinkle with oregano and top with slices of tomato, pepperoni or cabanossi and olives. Sprinkle with cheese and bake at 190°C (375°F, gas mark 5) for 10 minutes or until pizzas are crisp and brown.

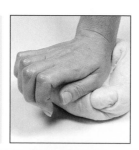

PREPARATION TIME
40 minutes

COOKING TIME
**10 minutes plus
1¹/₂ hours resting**

NUTRITIONAL VALUE PER SERVE   FAT **9.2** G   CARBOHYDRATE **15.8** G   PROTEIN **6.2** G

Spring rolls

INGREDIENTS

2 tablespoons oil
2 teaspoons finely chopped
  fresh ginger
1 small onion, finely chopped
500 g (1 lb) chicken stir-fry pieces,
  finely chopped
1/2 Chinese cabbage, finely chopped
1/2 red capsicum (pepper),
  seeded and thinly sliced
4 mushrooms, thinly sliced
2 teaspoons cornflour
1 tablespoon water
1 tablespoon soy sauce
1 packet large spring roll wrappers
oil for deep frying
dipping sauce
125 g (4 oz) apricot jam
1 tablespoon lemon juice
2 tablespoons white vinegar
1 tablespoon soy sauce
1 tablespoon water
makes 32

PREPARATION TIME
40 minutes

COOKING TIME
40 minutes

1 In a frying pan, place apricot jam, lemon juice, white vinegar, 1 tablespoon soy sauce and 1 tablespoon water. Mix all ingredients together, and heat gently while stirring. Set aside.

2 In the wok add 2 tablespoons oil and heat. Add ginger and onion and stir-fry until onion is pale gold in colour. Add chicken and stir-fry about 2 minutes until white. Toss in cabbage, capsicum (pepper) and mushrooms and stir-fry for 1 minute, mixing chicken through the vegetables. In a small bowl, combine cornflour and water.

3 Add soy sauce and 2 tablespoons of dipping sauce to the wok, tossing to mix through. Push the ingredients to one side of the wok and add blended cornflour to the juices in the base of the wok. As juices thicken, stir and toss through the vegetables. Remove from heat and spread mixture out onto a flat tray to cool. Wrap 1 heaped tablespoon chicken mixture in each wrapper according to packet directions.

4 Wipe out the wok, heat and add fresh oil to approximately 5 cm (2 in) deep. Heat oil and fry rolls a few at a time until golden and crisp. Drain on absorbent paper. Serve hot with dipping sauce.

Tip: Mini spring rolls are ideal finger food for a crowd. Cut spring roll wrappers in half and use 2 teaspoons spring roll mixture. Place mixture on bottom end of strip and roll once. Fold in side and continue to roll. Seal end with a little egg white. Serve with dipping sauce.

NUTRITIONAL VALUE PER SERVE	FAT **13.7** G	CARBOHYDRATE **15.7** G	PROTEIN **8.6** G

Dim sims

INGREDIENTS

100 g (3½ oz) prawns (shrimps),
  peeled
4 shallots, cut into 2.5 cm (1 in)
  lengths
125 g (4 oz) pork mince
⅛ small cabbage, finely chopped
1 egg
2 tablespoons soy sauce
few drops sesame oil
½ teaspoon salt
1 tablespoon cornflour
1 packet won ton wrappers
oil for deep frying
makes about 30

PREPARATION TIME
25 minutes

COOKING TIME
30 minutes

1 In a food processor, place prawns (shrimps) and shallots and process until well combined. Add pork, cabbage, egg, soy sauce, sesame oil, salt and cornflour. Process until well-combined.

2 Place a teaspoon of mixture into the centre of each won ton wrapper. Pinch the won ton skin together at the top to form a small package.

3 In a wok, heat 5 cm (2 in) oil and cook dim sims in batches, about 4–5 minutes until golden and cooked through.

4 Drain on kitchen paper and serve with soy sauce or your favourite dipping sauce.

NUTRITIONAL VALUE PER SERVE	FAT 25 G	CARBOHYDRATE 7.7 G	PROTEIN 6.4 G

Lobster filo triangles

INGREDIENTS

8 sheets filo pastry
125 g (4 oz) butter, melted and cooled
lobster cream filling
1 cooked lobster
3 tablespoons butter
6 spring onions (green onions),
  chopped
2 cloves garlic, crushed
1½ tablespoons plain flour
4 tablespoons white wine
4 tablespoons thick cream
pinch cayenne pepper
freshly ground black pepper
makes 32

PREPARATION TIME
40 minutes

COOKING TIME
25 minutes

1 To make filling, remove meat from lobster, chop finely and set aside. Melt 3 tablespoons butter in a saucepan over a medium heat. Add spring onions (green onions) and garlic and cook, stirring, until onions are tender. Stir in flour and cook for 1 minute.

2 Remove pan from heat and whisk in wine and cream, a little at a time, until well blended. Season to taste with cayenne and black pepper, return to heat and cook, stirring constantly, until sauce boils and thickens. Reduce heat to low and simmer for 3 minutes. Remove from heat, stir in lobster meat and cool completely.

3 Preheat oven to 220°C (425°F, gas mark 7). Cut pastry sheets lengthwise into 5 cm (2 in) strips. Working with one strip of pastry at a time, brush pastry with melted butter. Place a teaspoonful of the filling at one end of strip, fold corner of pastry diagonally over filling, then continue folding diagonally up the strip to make a neat triangle.

4 Place triangles on a lightly greased baking tray, brush with butter and bake for 10–15 minutes or until golden.

NUTRITIONAL VALUE PER SERVE	FAT **17.8** G	CARBOHYDRATE **7.8** G	PROTEIN **11.6** G

Smoked salmon carpaccio

INGREDIENTS

4 tablespoons extra virgin olive oil
45 ml (1½ fl oz) lemon juice
1 small red onion, finely chopped
2 teaspoons small whole capers
350 g (1–1½ oz) smoked salmon
1 tablespoon roughly
   chopped parsley
black pepper, freshly ground
extra capers for garnish
serves 4

PREPARATION TIME
15 minutes

1 In a large bowl, combine oil, lemon juice, onion and capers. Whisk
   to combine and set aside.

2 Arrange smoked salmon on serving plates.

3 Drizzle the dressing over the smoked salmon, sprinkle with
   parsley and ground black pepper, and serve. Garnish with extra
   capers.

NUTRITIONAL VALUE PER SERVE	FAT 16.9 G	CARBOHYDRATE 1.1 G	PROTEIN 15.3 G

Baked ricotta mushrooms

INGREDIENTS

10 large mushrooms,
  stems removed
1 tablespoon grated
  parmesan cheese
1 tablespoon dried breadcrumbs
ricotta and herb filling
125 g (4 oz) ricotta cheese
3 sun-dried tomatoes, soaked in
  warm water until soft, chopped
1 tablespoon finely diced red onion
1 tablespoon chopped fresh basil
1 tablespoon snipped fresh chives
1 teaspoon lemon juice
freshly ground black pepper
makes 10

PREPARATION TIME
15 minutes

COOKING TIME
15 minutes

1 Preheat oven to 180°C (350°F, gas mark 4). Line a baking tray with
non-stick baking paper. Set aside.

2 In a large bowl, place ricotta, tomatoes, onion, basil, chives, lemon
juice and black pepper to taste. Mix to combine.

3 Spoon filling into mushroom caps and place on prepared baking
tray. Combine parmesan and breadcrumbs. Sprinkle over
mushrooms. Bake for 10–15 minutes or until filling is set and top
is golden.

NUTRITIONAL VALUE PER SERVE	FAT 5.4 G	CARBOHYDRATE 8.6 G	PROTEIN 7 G

Roasted capsicum with feta and olives

INGREDIENTS

2 large red capsicums (peppers)
   halved and seeded
2 baby aubergines (eggplants), sliced
60 g (2 oz) semi sun-dried tomatoes
60 g (2 oz) olives
100 g (3¹/₂ oz) Greek feta, cubed
2 tablespoons olive oil
2 teaspoons fresh oregano leaves
1 clove garlic, crushed
serves 4

PREPARATION TIME
15 minutes

COOKING TIME
20–25 minutes

1 Preheat oven to 180°C (350°F, gas mark 4).

2 Place capsicums (peppers) on a lightly greased baking tray, skin-side down. Place aubergine (eggplant) slices, tomatoes, olives and feta inside capsicums (peppers).

3 In a jar, mix together olive oil, oregano and garlic. Drizzle this oil mixture over capsicums (peppers), and bake for 20–25 minutes.

NUTRITIONAL VALUE PER SERVE	FAT 7.2 G	CARBOHYDRATE 6 G	PROTEIN 3.6 G

Pork apple parcels

INGREDIENTS

800 g (1 lb 10 oz) lean pork schnitzel,
  trimmed of fat, pounded
  until very thin
2 Granny Smith apples, chopped
60 g (2 oz) sultanas
juice of ½ lemon
½ cup (125 ml, 4 fl oz) plum sauce
½ cup (125 ml , 4 fl oz) apple juice
1 tablespoon soy sauce
1 tablespoon honey
makes 12 parcels

PREPARATION TIME
15 minutes

COOKING TIME
25 minutes

1 Preheat oven to 180°C (350°F, gas mark 4). Cut pork into 10 cm (4 in)squares and set aside.

2 In a large bowl, place apples, sultanas and lemon juice. Mix to combine. Spread each pork square with plum sauce to within 2 cm (1 in) of the edges, reserving 2 tablespoons plum sauce for dipping. Place a small mound of the apple mixture in the centre. Roll up to form a parcel. Tie with cooking string. Place in a lightly greased casserole dish.

3 Combine apple juice, soy sauce and honey. Pour over pork parcels. Cover loosely with foil. Bake for 20–25 minutes or until pork is browned and tender. Remove parcels from casserole dish and stir 2 tablespoons plum sauce into cooking juices. Serve with parcels for dipping.

NUTRITIONAL VALUE PER SERVE   FAT **1.9** G   CARBOHYDRATE **13.1** G   PROTEIN **10.5** G

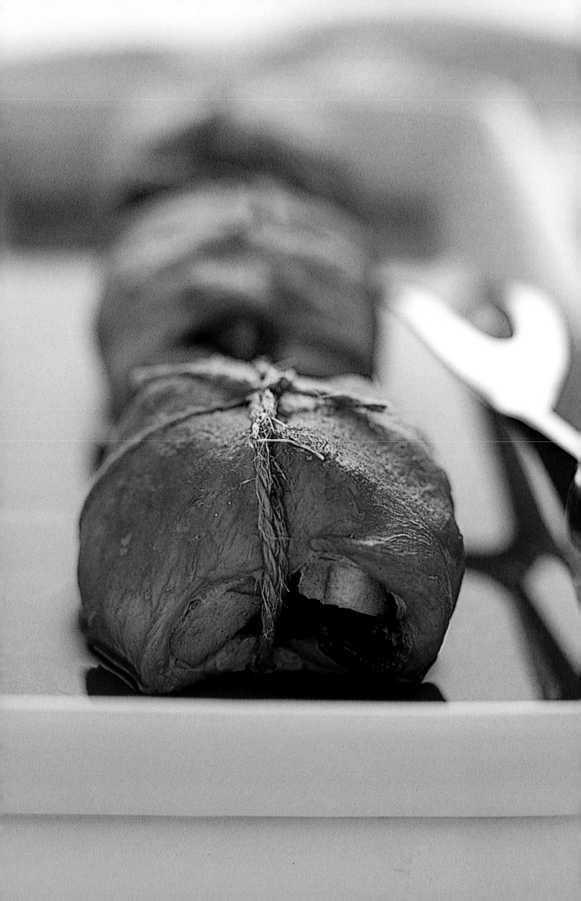

Moroccan lemon chicken shish kebabs

INGREDIENTS

500 g (1 lb) chicken breast fillets, trimmed of fat, cut into 2 cm (1 in) cubes

moroccan lemon marinade
1 tablespoon chopped parsley
1 tablespoon fresh rosemary leaves
2 teaspoons fresh thyme leaves
1 clove garlic, crushed
1 teaspoon black peppercorns, crushed
grated rind (zest) and juice of 1 lemon
1 tablespoon olive oil
8 large metal or bamboo skewers
makes 8 kebabs

1 In a non-metallic bowl, place parsley, rosemary, thyme, garlic, black pepper, lemon juice and rind and oil. Add chicken. Toss to combine. Cover and refrigerate for at least 30 minutes.

2 Preheat barbecue or grill to a high heat. If using bamboo skewers, soak in cold water for at least 20 minutes.

3 Thread chicken onto skewers. Place on barbecue grill or under grill. Cook, brushing frequently with marinade and turning, for 6–10 minutes or until chicken is cooked.

PREPARATION TIME
15 minutes, plus 30 minutes marinating

COOKING TIME
10 minutes

NUTRITIONAL VALUE PER SERVE	FAT 8.2 G	CARBOHYDRATE 0.2 G	PROTEIN 19.6 G

Chicken and mushroom vol-au-vents

INGREDIENTS

75 g (2½ oz) butter
8 mushrooms, sliced
4 spring onions (green onions), sliced
1 tablespoon chopped fresh parsley
350 g (11½ oz) chicken breast fillets, diced
1 tablespoon plain flour
75 ml (2½ fl oz) carrot juice
1 tablespoon celery juice
1 tablespoon red capsicum (pepper) juice
100 ml (3½ fl oz) chicken stock
½ cup (125 ml, 4 fl oz) wine
salt and pepper
4 large vol-au-vent cases
makes 4 large vol-au-vents

1 Preheat oven to 190°C (375°F, gas mark 5). Heat 25 g (¾ oz) butter in a large frying pan and sauté mushrooms, spring onions (green onions) and parsley on medium heat for 3–4 minutes. Remove from pan and set aside.

2 Add remaining butter and cook the chicken for 3–4 minutes until browned. Add flour, stir, then add vegetable juices, stock, wine and salt and pepper. Bring to the boil, reduce heat, add mushroom mixture and stir through.

3 Fill vol-au-vent cases with chicken mixture and place on a lightly oiled baking tray in the oven for 15 minutes until heated through. Serve immediately.

PREPARATION TIME
20 minutes

COOKING TIME
35 minutes

NUTRITIONAL VALUE PER SERVE   FAT 8.8 G   CARBOHYDRATE 3.1 G   PROTEIN 8.5 G

Salmon vegetable parcels

INGREDIENTS

1 small orange sweet potato,
  sliced lengthwise
1 large courgette (zucchini),
  sliced lengthwise
1 large carrot, sliced lengthwise
4 large silverbeet or English
  spinach leaves
4 x 150 g (5 oz) salmon or ocean trout
  fillets, skinned and boned
1 teaspoon chopped fresh oregano
1 tablespoon chopped fresh parsley
crushed fresh black peppercorns
2–3 sprigs fresh oregano
2–3 large sprigs fresh parsley
water for steaming
serves 4

PREPARATION TIME
25 minutes

COOKING TIME
25 minutes

1 In a large pan of boiling water, cook sweet
   potato, courgette (zucchini) and carrot until
   just tender. Drain well and set aside. Remove
   thick white stems from silverbeet, if using.
   Gently boil or microwave leaves until just
   wilted. Drain well and set aside.

2 Cut four pieces of plastic food wrap, each
   about 30 cm (12 in) long. Place on work surface.
   Place a silverbeet or spinach leaf on each piece
   of food wrap and overlap edges where the
   stem has been removed. Place a piece of fish in
   the centre of each leaf. Sprinkle with oregano,
   parsley and black pepper.

3 Cover fish with sweet potato, courgette
   (zucchini) and carrot slices. Wrap silverbeet
   around fish and vegetables to make parcels.
   Wrap plastic food wrap around each parcel
   and tie ends in a knot to seal. Place on a plate.
   Cover and refrigerate until ready to cook.

4 In a wok, place oregano and parsley sprigs and
   5 cm (2in) of water. Bring to simmering. Place
   fish parcels in a bamboo steamer and then
   place steamer over wok. Cover. Steam for
   10 minutes or until fish just starts to flake
   when pressed with a fork – the cooked fish
   should still be pink inside.

5 To serve, remove and dispose of plastic wrap,
   and accompany fish parcels with steamed rice
   or potatoes and steamed vegetables of your
   choice.

NUTRITIONAL VALUE PER SERVE	FAT 3.9 G	CARBOHYDRATE 2.5 G	PROTEIN 11.3 G

Marinated calamari with a lemon and herb dressing

INGREDIENTS

90 ml (3 fl oz) lemon juice
3 cloves garlic, crushed
½ cup (125 ml, 4 fl oz) olive oil
1 kg (2 lb) calamari (squid),
  cut into thin rings
dressing
4 tablespoons lemon juice
90 ml (3 fl oz) olive oil
1½ tablespoons chopped
  fresh parsley
1 clove garlic, crushed
1 teaspoon dijon mustard
salt and pepper
serves 4–6

1 In a large glass dish, place 90 ml (3 fl oz) lemon juice, 3 cloves garlic and ½ cup (125 ml, 4 fl oz) oil. Add calamari, cover and refrigerate for 3 hours or overnight.

2 For the dressing: Place all ingredients in a large bowl or jar and whisk well, until thickened.

3 Heat a large pan or wok over a high heat and cook calamari 2–3 minutes until just cooked. Serve calamari drizzled with dressing.

PREPARATION TIME
**10 minutes, plus
3 hours or overnight
marinating**

COOKING TIME
5 minutes

NUTRITIONAL VALUE PER SERVE   FAT **10.1** G   CARBOHYDRATE **0.3** G   PROTEIN **13.5** G

Scallops baked with cured ham

INGREDIENTS

2 tablespoons olive oil
500 g (1 lb) scallops, in half shell
salt and freshly ground black pepper
1 small onion, finely chopped
1 clove garlic, crushed
60 g (2 oz) minced cured ham,
  such as proscuitto
3 tablespoons dry white wine
60 g (2 oz) breadcrumbs
1 tablespoon chopped parsley
1 teaspoon lemon juice
serves 2

1 Preheat oven to 200°C (400°C, gas mark 6). Heat 1 tablespoon oil in a large frying pan and sauté scallops over high heat for 1 minute. Divide the scallops among the shells and sprinkle with salt and pepper.

2 Add the onion and garlic and a little more oil, if necessary, to the frying pan. Cover and cook over low heat for 15 minutes. Add the ham and sauté for 1 minute. Stir in wine and let it cook off. Spoon mixture over scallops.

3 In a small bowl, combine the bread crumbs, parsley, lemon juice and remaining oil. Sprinkle over the scallops. Place shells on baking sheet and bake 10 minutes. If necessary, put under the grill to brown the top.

PREPARATION TIME
15 minutes

COOKING TIME
30 minutes

NUTRITIONAL VALUE PER SERVE	FAT **5.9** G	CARBOHYDRATE **5.7** G	PROTEIN **10.1** G

Thai prawn cakes

INGREDIENTS

500 g (1 lb) uncooked peeled prawns
  (shrimps), deveined
2 spring onions (green onions),
  chopped
1 teaspoon finely chopped
  lemongrass
2 kaffir lime or lemon myrtle leaves,
  soaked in boiling water for 15
  minutes, finely chopped (optional)
1 egg white
1 tablespoon fish sauce
1 tablespoon lime juice
1 teaspoon sweet chilli sauce or to taste
4 tablespoons fresh breadcrumbs
2 tablespoons chopped fresh mint
2 tablespoons chopped
  fresh coriander (cilantro)
coriander (cilantro) dipping sauce
2 tablespoons chopped
  fresh coriander (cilantro)
1 spring onion (green onion), finely
  chopped
1 clove garlic, crushed
1 teaspoon brown or palm sugar
4 tablespoons rice or sherry vinegar
1/2 teaspoon fish sauce
2 teaspoons low-salt soy sauce
1/2 teaspoon chilli sauce (optional)
**serves 4 as a main meal or
8 as a starter**

PREPARATION TIME
15–20 minutes,
plus 30 minutes
refrigeration

COOKING TIME
5–8 minutes

1 Place prawns (shrimps) in a food processor.
   Using the pulse button, process until roughly
   chopped. Add spring onions (green onions),
   lemongrass, lime leaves, egg white, fish sauce,
   lime juice and chilli sauce. Using the pulse
   button, process until just combined. Transfer
   mixture to a large bowl. Fold in breadcrumbs,
   mint and coriander (cilantro).

2 Shape mixture into 4 cm (1 1/2 in) round patties.
   Place on a plate lined with plastic food wrap
   or thread 2–3 patties on a lemongrass skewer
   (see cook's tip below). Cover. Refrigerate for
   30 minutes or until patties are firm.

3 Preheat a barbecue to a medium heat. Add
   patties. Cook for 2–3 minutes each side or until
   lightly browned. Alternatively, heat a non-
   stick frying pan over a medium heat. Lightly
   spray or brush with unsaturated oil and pan-
   fry, or cook under a medium grill or bake in the
   oven at 200°C (400°F, gas mark 6) – if baking
   do not thread onto lemongrass skewers.

4 For the dipping sauce: Place coriander
   (cilantro), spring onion (green onion), garlic,
   sugar, vinegar and fish, soy and chilli sauces in
   a bowl. Whisk to combine. Serve with prawn
   cakes for dipping.

Cook's tip: Crab or white fish fillets can be
used instead of prawns (shrimps) to make
these fish cakes. For an attractive presentation
and added flavour, thread prepared prawn
(shrimp) cakes onto fresh lemongrass
stems, then cook on the barbecue. Soak the
lemongrass stems in cold water for 1 hour
before using – this helps prevent the skewers
from burning during cooking.

NUTRITIONAL VALUE PER SERVE	FAT 6.3 G	CARBOHYDRATE 4.4 G	PROTEIN 14.5 G

Feta and ricotta stuffed tomatoes

INGREDIENTS

6 large firm tomatoes
150 g (5 oz) feta cheese, crumbed
150 g (5 oz) ricotta cheese
60 g (2 oz) pine nuts, chopped
10 black olives, pitted and chopped
1¹/₂ tablespoons chopped
   fresh oregano
3 tablespoons wholemeal
   breadcrumbs
freshly ground black pepper
6 black olives, to garnish
extra oregano leaves to garnish
serves 6

PREPARATION TIME
15–20 minutes

COOKING TIME
20–25 minutes

1 Preheat oven to 180°C (350°F, gas mark 4).

2 Cut a lid off the top of each tomato and set aside. Carefully scoop the centre of each tomato into a large bowl. Combine half the tomato mixture with the feta, ricotta, pine nuts, olives, oregano, breadcrumbs and pepper. Beat mixture together, and spoon back into the cases (piling the tops high). Discard left over tomato flesh.

3 Place in a lightly greased shallow oven-proof dish and bake for 20–25 minutes.

4 Garnish with an olive and oregano and serve immediately.

NUTRITIONAL VALUE PER SERVE	FAT 6.2 G	CARBOHYDRATE 3.6 G	PROTEIN 4.2 G

Polenta and corn fritters

INGREDIENTS

1¹/₂ cups (375 ml, 12 fl oz) water
¹/₂ teaspoon salt
75 g (2¹/₂ oz) polenta
100 g (3¹/₂ oz) corn kernels
1 spring onion (green onion),
   finely sliced
1 tablespoon finely chopped parsley
1 clove garlic, crushed
45g (1¹/₂ oz) plain flour
¹/₂ teaspoon baking powder
1 egg, lightly beaten
pepper and salt to taste
4 tablespoons olive oil,
   enough to cover base of pan
makes 16

PREPARATION TIME
10 minutes

COOKING TIME
10–15 minutes

1 In a large pan, bring water and salt to boil. Gradually add polenta, stirring continuously
   for 3–5 minutes or until polenta becomes thick and comes together like glue.

2 Remove from heat and add corn, spring onion (green onion), parsley and garlic. Stir until
   combined. Transfer to a bowl and set aside to cool.

3 In a bowl, sift together flour and baking powder. Add to polenta and mix to combine.
   Add egg, salt and pepper and mix to combine.

4 Heat oil in a large pan on a medium-high heat. Place tablespoons of polenta mixture in
   pan and cook in batches for 1–2 minutes on each side until lightly browned. Serve
   hot or cold.

NUTRITIONAL VALUE PER SERVE	FAT 10.8 G	CARBOHYDRATE 9.2 G	PROTEIN 2.6 G

Potato feta fritters

INGREDIENTS

245 g (7½ oz) potato,
  cooked and mashed
125 g (4 oz) feta cheese, crumbled
1 egg, beaten
3 spring onions (green onions),
  chopped
3 tablespoons chopped fresh dill
1 tablespoon lemon juice
finely grated rind (zest) of ½ lemon
freshly ground black pepper
flour, for dredging
4 tablespoons olive oil
extra dill and lemon for garnish
serves 4

1 In a medium bowl, place the potato, feta, egg, spring onions (green onions), dill, lemon juice, rind and black pepper. Mix until well combined. Cover and refrigerate for 1–2 hours until firm.

2 Roll the mixture into golf ball-sized fritters, and flatten slightly. Dredge lightly in flour, using a small sieve.

3 Heat olive oil in a large frying pan. Cook fritters in batches for about 3–5 minutes until golden brown on both sides. Drain on a paper towel and serve immediately. Garnish with extra dill and lemon.

PREPARATION TIME
10 minutes, plus
1–2 hours refrigeration

COOKING TIME
15 minutes

NUTRITIONAL VALUE PER SERVE	FAT 19.8 G	CARBOHYDRATE 5.9 G	PROTEIN 6.4 G

Roast pumpkin, potato and rosemary frittatas

INGREDIENTS

300 g (10 oz) butternut pumpkin,
  peeled, seeded and diced
  into 2 cm (1 in) pieces
220 g (7½ oz) potatoes, peeled
  and diced into 2 cm (1 in) pieces
220 g (7½ oz) sweet potatoes, peeled
  and diced into 2 cm (1 in) pieces
1 tablespoon olive oil
2 sprigs rosemary, roughly chopped
½ teaspoon sea salt
4 eggs
½ cup (125 ml, 4 fl oz) cream
½ cup (125 ml, 4 fl oz) milk
1 clove garlic, crushed
60 g (2 oz) parmesan cheese, grated
salt and pepper to taste
serves 4

1 Preheat oven to 220°C (425°F, gas mark 7). Place pumpkin, potato, sweet potato, oil, half the rosemary and sea salt in a baking dish. Toss and bake for 20 minutes or until just cooked. Remove from oven and set aside.

2 Grease a 12 x 1 cup (250 ml, 8 fl oz) capacity muffin tin. Line bases with baking paper.

3 In a large bowl, combine eggs, cream, milk, garlic, parmesan, remaining rosemary and salt and pepper. Add potato, pumpkin and sweet potato. Reduce oven to 180°C (350°F, gas mark 4).

4 Pour mixture into muffin tins and bake for 30–35 minutes.

PREPARATION TIME
15 minutes

COOKING TIME
55 minutes

NUTRITIONAL VALUE PER SERVE   FAT **9.2** G   CARBOHYDRATE **6.7** G   PROTEIN **5.7** G

Glossary

Al dente: Italian term to describe pasta and rice that are cooked until tender but still firm to the bite.

Bake blind: to bake pastry cases without their fillings. Line the raw pastry case with greaseproof paper and fill with raw rice or dried beans to prevent collapsed sides and puffed base. Remove paper and fill 5 minutes before completion of cooking time.

Baste: to spoon hot cooking liquid over food at intervals during cooking to moisten and flavour it.

Beat: to make a mixture smooth with rapid and regular motions using a spatula, wire whisk or electric mixer; to make a mixture light and smooth by enclosing air.

Beurre manié: equal quantities of butter and flour mixed together to a smooth paste and stirred bit by bit into a soup, stew or sauce while on the heat to thicken. Stop adding when desired thickness results.

Bind: to add egg or a thick sauce to hold ingredients together when cooked.

Blanch: to plunge some foods into boiling water for less than a minute and immediately plunge into iced water. This is to brighten the colour of some vegetables and to remove skin from tomatoes and nuts.

Blend: to mix 2 or more ingredients thoroughly together; do not confuse with blending in an electric blender.

Boil: to cook in a liquid brought to boiling point and kept there.

Boiling point: when bubbles rise continually and break over the entire surface of the liquid, reaching a temperature of 100°C (212°F). In some cases food is held at this high temperature for a few seconds then heat is turned to low for slower cooking. See *simmer*.

Bouquet garni: a bundle of several herbs tied together with string for easy removal, placed into pots of stock, soups and stews for flavour. A few sprigs of fresh thyme, parsley and bay leaf are used. Can be purchased in sachet form for convenience.

Caramelise: to heat sugar in a heavy-based pan until it liquefies and develops a caramel colour. Vegetables such as blanched carrots and sautéed onions may be sprinkled with sugar and caramelised.

Chill: to place in the refrigerator or stir over ice until cold.

Clarify: to make a liquid clear by removing sediments and impurities. To melt fat and remove any sediment.

Coat: to dust or roll food items in flour to cover the surface before the food is cooked. Also, to coat in flour, egg and breadcrumbs.

Cool: to stand at room temperature until some or all heat is removed, eg cool a little, cool completely.

Cream: to make creamy and fluffy by working the mixture with the back of a wooden spoon; usually refers to creaming butter and sugar or margarine. May also be done with an electric mixer.

Croutons: small cubes of bread, toasted or fried, used as an addition to salads or as a garnish to soups and stews.

Crudités: raw vegetable sticks served with a dipping sauce.

Crumb: to coat foods in flour, egg and breadcrumbs to form a protective coating for foods which are fried. Also adds flavour and texture and enhances appearance.

Cube: to cut into small pieces with six even sides, eg cubes of meat.

Cut in: to combine fat, such as butter or shortening, and flour using 2 knives scissor-fashion or a pastry blender, to make pastry.

Deglaze: to dissolve dried-out cooking juices left on the base and sides of a roasting dish or frying pan. Add a little water, wine or stock, scrape and stir over heat until dissolved. Resulting liquid is used to make a flavoursome gravy or added to a sauce or casserole.

Degrease: to skim fat from the surface of cooking liquids, eg stocks, soups, casseroles.

Dice: to cut into small cubes.

Dredge: to heavily coat with icing sugar, sugar, flour or cornflour.

Dressing: a mixture added to completed dishes to add moisture and flavour, eg salads, cooked vegetables.

Drizzle: to pour in a fine thread-like stream moving over a surface.

Egg wash: beaten egg with milk or water used to brush over pastry, bread dough or biscuits to give a sheen and golden brown colour.

Essence: a strong flavouring liquid, usually made by distillation. Only a few drops are needed to flavour.

Fillet: a piece of prime meat, fish or poultry which is boneless or has all bones removed.

Flake: to separate cooked fish into flakes, removing any bones and skin, using 2 forks.

Flame: to ignite warmed alcohol over food or to pour into a pan with food, ignite, then serve.

Flute: to make decorative indentations around the pastry rim before baking.

Fold in: combining of a light, whisked or creamed mixture with other ingredients. Add a portion of the other ingredients at a time and mix using a gentle circular motion, over and under the mixture so that air will not be lost. Use a metal spoon or spatula.

Glaze: to brush or coat food with a liquid that will give the finished product a glossy appearance, and on baked products, a golden brown colour.

Grease: to rub the surface of a metal or heatproof dish with oil or fat, to prevent the food from sticking.

Herbed butter: softened butter mixed with finely chopped fresh herbs and re-chilled. Used to serve on grilled meats and fish.

Hors d'oeuvre: small savoury foods served as an appetiser, popularly known today as 'finger food'.

Infuse: to steep foods in a liquid until the liquid absorbs their flavour.

Joint: to cut poultry and game into serving pieces by dividing at the joint.

Julienne: to cut some food, eg vegetables and processed meats, into fine strips the length of matchsticks. Used in salads or as a garnish to cooked dishes.

Knead: to work a yeast dough in a pressing, stretching and folding motion with the heel of the hand until smooth and elastic to develop the gluten strands. Non-yeast doughs should be lightly and quickly handled as gluten development is not desired.

Line: to cover the inside of a baking tin with paper for the easy removal of the cooked product from the baking tin.

Macerate: to stand fruit in a syrup, liqueur or spirit to give added flavour.

Marinade: a flavoured liquid, into which food is placed for some time to give it flavour and to tenderise. Marinades include an acid ingredient such as vinegar or wine, oil and seasonings.

Mask: to evenly cover cooked food portions with a sauce, mayonnaise or savoury jelly.

Pan-fry: to fry foods in a small amount of fat or oil, sufficient to coat the base of the pan.

Parboil: to boil until partially cooked. The food is then finished by some other method.

Pare: to peel the skin from vegetables and fruit. 'Peel' is the popular term but 'pare' is the name given to the knife used; paring knife.

Pit: to remove stones or seeds from olives, cherries, dates.

Pith: the white lining between the rind and flesh of oranges, grapefruit and lemons.

Pitted: the olives, cherries, dates etc. with the stone removed, eg purchase pitted dates.

Poach: to simmer gently in enough hot liquid to almost cover the food so its shape will be retained.

Pound: to flatten meats with a meat mallet; to reduce to a paste or small particles with a mortar and pestle.

Simmer: to cook in liquid just below boiling point at about 96°C (205°F) with small bubbles rising gently to the surface.

Skim: to remove fat or froth from the surface of simmering food.

Stock: the liquid produced when meat, poultry, fish or vegetables have been simmered in water to extract the flavour. Used as a base for soups, sauces, casseroles etc. Convenience stock products are available.

Sweat: to cook sliced onions or vegetables in a small amount of butter in a covered pan over low heat, to soften them and release flavour without colouring.

Conversions

Measurements differ from country to country, so it's important to understand what the differences are. This Measurements Guide gives you simple 'at-a-glance' information for using the recipes in this book, wherever you may be.

Cooking is not an exact science – minor variations in measurements won't make a difference to your cooking.

EQUIPMENT

There is a difference in the size of measuring cups used internationally, but the difference is minimal (only 2–3 teaspoons). We use the Australian standard metric measurements in our recipes:

1 teaspoon.....5 ml	1 tablespoon.....20 ml
1/2 cup.....125 ml	1 cup.....250 ml
4 cups.....1 litre	

Measuring cups come in sets of one cup (250 ml), 1/2 cup (125 ml), 1/3 cup (80 ml) and 1/4 cup (60 ml). Use these for measuring liquids and certain dry ingredients.

Measuring spoons come in a set of four and should be used for measuring dry and liquid ingredients.

When using cup or spoon measures, always make them level (unless the recipe indicates otherwise).

DRY VERSUS WET INGREDIENTS

While this system of measures is consistent for liquids, it's more difficult to quantify dry ingredients. For instance, one level cup equals: 200 g of brown sugar; 210 g of caster sugar; and 110 g of icing sugar.

When measuring dry ingredients such as flour, don't push the flour down or shake it into the cup. It is best just to spoon the flour in until it reaches the desired amount. When measuring liquids, use a clear vessel indicating metric levels.

Always use medium eggs (55–60 g) when eggs are required in a recipe.

OVEN

Your oven should always be at the right temperature before placing the food in it to be cooked. Note that if your oven doesn't have a fan you may need to cook food for a little longer.

MICROWAVE

It is difficult to give an exact cooking time for microwave cooking. It is best to watch what you are cooking closely to monitor its progress.

STANDING TIME

Many foods continue to cook when you take them out of the oven or microwave. If a recipe states that the food needs to 'stand' after cooking, be sure not to overcook the dish.

CAN SIZES

The can sizes available in your supermarket or grocery store may not be the same as specified in the recipe. Don't worry if there is a small variation in size – it's unlikely to make a difference to the end result.

dry		liquids	
metric (grams)	imperial (ounces)	metric (millilitres)	imperial (fluid ounces)
		30 ml	1 fl oz
30 g	1 oz	60 ml	2 fl oz
60 g	2 oz	90 ml	3 fl oz
90 g	3 oz	100 ml	3 1/2 fl oz
100 g	3 1/2 oz	125 ml	4 fl oz
125 g	4 oz	150 ml	5 fl oz
150 g	5 oz	190 ml	6 fl oz
185 g	6 oz	250 ml	8 fl oz
200 g	7 oz	300 ml	10 fl oz
250 g	8 oz	500 ml	16 fl oz
280 g	9 oz	600 ml	20 fl oz (1 pint)*
315 g	10 oz	1000 ml (1 litre)	32 fl oz
330 g	11 oz		
370 g	12 oz		
400 g	13 oz		
440 g	14 oz		
470 g	15 oz		
500 g	16 oz (1 lb)		
750 g	24 oz (1 1/2 lb)		
1000 g (1 kg)	32 oz (2 lb)		*Note: an American pint is 16 fl oz.

cooking temperatures	°C (celsius)	°F (fahrenheit)	gas mark
very slow	120	250	1/2
slow	150	300	2
moderately slow	160	315	2–3
moderate	180	350	4
moderately hot	190	375	5
	200	400	6
hot	220	425	7
very hot	230	450	8
	240	475	9
	250	500	10

Index

Essential COOKING SERIES

COMPREHENSIVE, STEP-BY-STEP COOKING

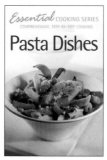

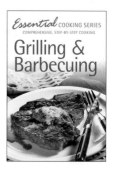

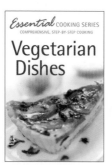

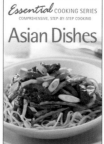